Deliverance According to

JUDE

Ebenezer Gabriels

Abigail Ebenezer-Gabriels

THE LORD GOD OF DELIVERANCE
The God of Israel
Save by the strength Your Right Hand

Introduction to the book of

Jude

The written message is a crucial component of deliverance. JUDE, the writer of the letter, introduces himself as a "bond-servant" of Jesus. In the writings of Jude, you will find deliverance, restoration and the power of the Lord. In this study, you will learn the principles and rules of deliverance, you will learn that as God's called and chosen vessel you must remain open to the deliverance power of the Lord.

Featuring

- ★ Jude's Principles of Deliverance
- ★ Jude's Principles of Deliverance
- ★ Jude's Principles of Deliverance
- ★ Jude's Principles of Deliverance
- ★ Jude's Principles of Deliverance

Deliverance in the Book of Jude

- ★ 9 Deliverance Discussions
- ★ Deliverance Highlights
- ★ Learning Journals
- ★ Jude's Prayers of Deliverance

Discussion 1

The book of Jude

Chapter 1 Verse 1

1

Jude,

a bondservant of Jesus Christ, and brother of James,

To those who are called, sanctified by God the Father, and preserved in Jesus Christ

#1

Jude's Principle of Targeted Deliverance

The message of deliverance is targeted to a specific audience, and the leader of deliverance understands that this message should be sent to the right audience.

This principle is found in Jude's opening address.

From: Jude

To: God's Anointed, God's Chosen, Carriers of God's Purpose, The Delivered, God's special People

Subject: A Message of Deliverance

Jude's Principle of Conceptualized Deliverance

Jude's introduction leads us into the concept of Bond Servanthood.

Who is a bond-servant?

A bondservant - Someone whose heart is undetachable from serving and helping others. In Jude's situation, he introduces himself, describing his commitment as a loyal follower of Jesus. In the simple introduction of his letter, he also reminds the reader of his association with James.

Who are the "called"?

The Called - Those who are beckoned to, and invited to the Father's special Presence. Those who are carrying God's special purpose within them. The called are leaders who are called to bring others into deliverance into the land of purpose.

#3

Jude's Principle of Authority in deliverance

Know your master

Deliverance requires that the ones communicating the message of deliverance have a tight-knitted relationship with Jesus, and use the authority from that relationship at all times, including when communicating.

Declare your allegiance

Jude's introduction gives us instant understanding that Jude's allegiance is to the Lord Jesus. His declaration of his allegiance to the Lord Jesus silences any threats or imagination seeking to question his spiritual authority.

Jude's message was to a unique audience - those who are called and loved. Those who have been called to fulfill a special assignment of the Lord, here on earth. Today that would be leaders in all areas - leaders in family, community, government, church, marketplace industries.

★ **Jude's Deliverance highlights**

- The message of deliverance
- God sends the message of deliverance to His people
- Every message of deliverance has a purpose
- Every deliverance message is specific

★ **Deliverance Prayer sets from the Book of Jude**

- Lord, qualify me as your called
- Preserve me in Jesus
- I declare my allegiance to the Lord Jesus
- I am of Jesus, I know that and Jesus knows me as His

Book of Jude Learning Journal

Discussion 2

The Book of Jude

Chapter 1 Verse 2

2

Mercy, peace, and love be multiplied to you.

#4

Jude's Principle of Prayer-first in Deliverance

Prayer first in deliverance gives leaders the opportunity to function on higher realms, and conquered grounds, rather than having to go into war zones.

> **Open all communication doors with prayers**: All types of communication doors, written or verbal, must be opened with prayers.

> **Prayer First**: Praying brings us into the place of hiding in the name of Jesus, and benefitting from the finished works of Jesus Christ, that we do not have to go into battle, when the power of prayers first is available.

While taking the prayer first approach, we are assured that the attention of the Lord is being brought into situations, and the help of heaven has been received.

★ **Jude's Deliverance highlights**

- The message of deliverance.
- God sends the message of deliverance to His people.
- Every message of deliverance has a purpose.

★ **Jude's Deliverance Prayer sets**
- Lord Jesus, teach me the ways of your deliverance.
- Lord Jesus, give me the power of communication to hear from you.

#5

Jude's Principle of Purposeful Prayers in deliverance

Purposeful prayers are prayers targeted to help meet a specific purpose. There were three areas of requests as seen in Jude's prayer.

The Prayer for Mercy

He prayed for mercy. Mercy is needed when people are brought to the place of judgment, especially if they are deserving of condemnation. The power of God's mercy comes to deliver.

The Prayer for love

In place of hate, Jude prays for the multiplication of love.

Purposeful prayers are led by the Holy Spirit. Flesh-inspired prayers are prayers prayed amiss, and are not purposeful, as it serves no purpose targeted to help meet a specific purpose.

Jude's Deliverance highlights

Purposeful prayer

★ **Deliverance Prayer sets from the Book of Jude**

- ○ Lord, qualify me as your called
- ○ Preserve me in Jesus
- ○ I declare my allegiance to the Lord Jesus
- ○ I am of Jesus, I know that and Jesus knows me as His

Book of Jude Learning Journal

Discussion 3

The Book of Jude

Chapter 1 Verse 3-4

3

Beloved, while I was very diligent to write to you concerning our common salvation, I found it necessary to write to you exhorting you to contend earnestly for the faith which was once for all delivered to the saints.

4

For certain men have crept in unnoticed, who long ago were marked out for this condemnation, ungodly men, who turn the grace of our God into lewdness and deny the only Lord God and our Lord Jesus Christ..

#6

Jude's Principles of diligence in deliverance

Diligence is the deliverance leader's companion. Jude exemplified diligence himself as he noted, "while I was very diligent" in his writing. He observed and understood through thoughts and considerations which are elements of diligence. He, then, found a strong reason to communicate with the leaders of deliverance.

Jude's Principles of observation in deliverance

Observation is one of the core principles of walking in God's deliverance. Jude observed an infiltration that was "unnoticed" and sounded the alarm, to call the attention of others in faith to a rising satanic and destructive trend which brings perversion.

> For certain men have crept in unnoticed, who long ago were marked out for this condemnation, ungodly men, who turn the grace of our God into lewdness and deny the only Lord God and our Lord Jesus Christ.

★ **Jude's Deliverance highlights**
  ○ Live diligently

- Live in observation

★ **Jude's Deliverance highlights**
- Lord Jesus, give me the gift of diligence.
- Lord Jesus, give me the gift of observation.

Book of Jude Learning Journal

_____
_____
_____
_____
_____
_____
_____
_____
_____
_____
_____
_____
_____
_____
_____
_____
_____
_____
_____
_____
_____
_____
_____
_____
_____

Discussion 4

Jude

Chapter 1 Verse **5-7**

5

But I want to remind you, though you once knew this, that the Lord, having saved the people out of the land of Egypt, afterward destroyed those who did not believe.

6

And the angels who did not keep their proper domain, but left their own abode, He has reserved in everlasting chains under darkness for the judgment of the great day;

7

as Sodom and Gomorrah, and the cities around them in a similar manner to these, having given themselves over to sexual immorality and gone after strange flesh, are set forth as an example, suffering the vengeance of eternal fire.

#7

Jude's Principles of faith in deliverance

Faith is one of the founding principles of deliverance. Faithlessness brings hardship to deliverance. Believers must hold firm to God's voice which will scale them through hard times.

Jude's Principles of maintenance of assigned domain in deliverance

Where is your primary place of assignment?
Everyone, even angels have their assigned place. When found, we must learn to keep our proper domains. Slavery and captivity lie in wait for those who go outside their God-given authoritized boundaries.

Jude's Principles of abstinence from communal suffering in Deliverance

Everyone, even angels have their assigned place. When found, we must learn to keep our proper domains. Slavery and captivity lie in wait for those who go outside their God-given authoritized boundaries.

★ **Jude's Deliverance Highlights**
- ○ The power of faith.
- ○ The power in assigned spaces.
- ○ The power of boundaries in deliverance.

★ **Jude's Deliverance Prayersets**
- ○ Lord Jesus, give me the power to stay in my God given domain, in the name of Jesus.
- ○ Lord Jesus, give me the understanding of boundaries in deliverance.

Discussion 5

Jude

Chapter 1 Verse 8-11

8

Likewise also these dreamers defile the flesh, reject authority, and speak evil of dignitaries.

9

Yet Michael the archangel, in contending with the devil, when he disputed about the body of Moses, dared not bring against him a reviling accusation, but said, "The Lord rebuke you!"

10

But these speak evil of whatever they do not know; and whatever they know naturally, like brute beasts, in these things they corrupt themselves.

11

Woe to them! For they have gone in the way of Cain, have run greedily in the error of Balaam for profit, and perished in the rebellion of Korah

#7

Jude's Principles of Honoring Authority in Deliverance

Honor is one of the gateways to deliverance. The rejection of authority and speaking falsely against authority is dishonorable, and the Lord frowns at it.

Jude's Principles of God's Overruling in Deliverance

When deliverance leaders are faced with hard battles, and there is nowhere to turn, there are the warring angels calling for the Lord's rebuke upon the devil. There is no place for pride in deliverance, but there is always the name of the Lord to run into when help is needed.

Jude's Principles of Staying Steadfast in God in Deliverance

There are ways that displease the Lord, these are the ways of Cain whose sacrifice was not accepted, and those who work in greed. Greed brings error, and also rebellion, the Lord hates. In deliverance, God's people are to depart from the ways of rebellion, greed and ungratefulness, as these are major blockers of deliverance.

- ★ **Jude's Deliverance Highlights**
    - ○ The power of staying out of the pits of greed and rebellion.
    - ○ The power in submission to authorities.

- ★ **Jude's Deliverance Prayersets**
    - ○ Lord Jesus, visit me with your honor.
    - ○ Lord Jesus, give me a heart that is steady.

_____
_____
_____
_____
_____
_____
_____
_____
_____
_____
_____
_____
_____
_____
_____
_____
_____
_____
_____
_____
_____
_____
_____
_____

Discussion 6

12

These are spots in your love feasts, while they feast with you without fear, serving only themselves. They are clouds without water, carried about by the winds; late autumn trees without fruit, twice dead, pulled up by the roots;

13

raging waves of the sea, foaming up their own shame; wandering stars for whom is reserved the blackness of darkness forever.

14

Now Enoch, the seventh from Adam, prophesied about these men also, saying, "Behold, the Lord comes with ten thousands of His saints,

15

to execute judgment on all, to convict all who are ungodly among them of all their ungodly deeds which they have committed in an ungodly way, and of all the harsh things which ungodly sinners have spoken against Him

#7

Jude's Principles of Steadiness and Staying Grounded in deliverance

Substance is power in the place of deliverance. The lack of it is called emptiness. Clouds without rain display arrogance without something of Godly worth to back up arrogance claims. God's children are called to a life of power, and the demonstration of God's power, living a life worthy of the calling Jesus has called forth.

Jude's Principles of Godly Judgment in Deliverance

God brings justice across all forms of injustices at the right time. Pride brings shame, wandering, ungodliness invites the wrath of God. Substance is power in the place of deliverance. Where there is unending sin, judgment comes. God's children must not usurp God's grace because there is an end to that too.

- ★ **Jude's Deliverance highlights**
  - ○ The power of humility.
  - ○ The power of deliverance.
  - ○

- ★ **Jude's Deliverance highlights**
  - ○ Lord Jesus, bring me into the place of steadiness in deliverance.
  - ○ Lord Jesus, judge in my favor for my deliverance.

_____
_____
_____
_____
_____
_____
_____
_____
_____
_____
_____
_____
_____
_____
_____
_____
_____
_____
_____
_____
_____
_____
_____
_____
_____
_____
_____
_____

Discussion 7

Jude

Chapter 1 Verse 16-19

16
These are grumblers, complainers, walking according to their own lusts; and they mouth great swelling words, flattering people to gain advantage.

17
But you, beloved, remember the words which were spoken before by the apostles of our Lord Jesus Christ:

18
how they told you that there would be mockers in the last time who would walk according to their own ungodly lusts.

19
These are sensual persons, who cause divisions, not having the Spirit.

#8

Jude's Principles of Alertness in Deliverance

Tools of Satan to deceive God's children include: complain, lust, and sometimes flatter. God's children must stay alert, and filled with the Holy Spirit to wade off the enemy's resources.

The Apostles forewarned believers about this; this satanic practice continues to exist till date. How can believers handle this?

Alertness is the state of being aware and present. Staying alert ensures that you do not get lost, in spiritual battles, or the physical.

Grumbling and complaining is a spirit that accompanies the lack of gratitude. It is an anti-worship spirit that seeks to point fingers. This spirit also brings accusation, and you must learn to conquer this power

★ **Jude's Deliverance highlights**
- Stay alert in your mind that the spirit of complaints will not overshadow you.
- Get away from all appearances of evil and lustful desires.
- Understand the workings of the spirit of grumbling and complaining and nab it before it starts.

★ **Jude's Deliverance prayer sets**
- Lord Jesus, fill me with the power to overcome the spirit of lust
- Lord Jesus, fill me with the power to overcome the spirit of complaints.

Book of Jude Learning Journal

Discussion 8

The Book of Jude

Chapter 1 Verse **20-22**

20

But you, beloved, building yourselves up on your most holy faith, praying in the Holy Spirit,

21

keep yourselves in the love of God, looking for the mercy of our Lord Jesus Christ unto eternal life.

22

And on some have compassion, making a distinction;

23

but others save with fear, pulling them out of the fire, hating even the garment defiled by the flesh.

#9

Jude's Principles of Tongue-Speaking in Deliverance

Speaking in tongues has been an object of dissension in many churches - However the book of Jude advises that believers who are elect should pray in the tongues as it helps grow your spiritual stature.

Jude's Principles of Love in Deliverance

Love remains the currency of connecting with the Lord in deliverance. Through love, the greatest battle can be won. Everyone approaching deliverance must learn to preserve the love of God in their lives.

Jude's Principles of Delivering others in Deliverance

We are called to deliver others too, however possible. Every believer has been called to preach the message of salvation to the unsaved. This is such an urgent Word that requires that we snatch the unsaved out of the way of perdition.

★ **Jude's Deliverance highlights**
  - Speak in tongues, it's a second nature to deliverance
  - Love the Lord, and continue loving on Him, this is the only hope.
  - Show love to others too.

★ **Jude's Deliverance Prayer sets**
  - Lord, open my tongue into the deeper realm of you power.
  - Lord Jesus, display your love over my life.

Book of Jude Learning Journal

Discussion 9

The Book of Jude
Chapter 1 Verse 20-22

24

Now to Him who is able to keep you from stumbling,
And to present you faultless
Before the presence of His glory with exceeding joy,

25

To God our Savior,
Who alone is wise,
Be glory and majesty,
Dominion and power,
Both now and forever.
Amen.

.

#10

Jude's Principles of Purity in Deliverance

The Lord seeks to wash us clean and purify us. God's people must be open to the cleansing and satisfaction of the Lord, as the goal of this is to present you back to the Lord.

Jude's Principles of Worship in Deliverance

Worship has always been a part of deliverance - it's inseparable. Worship is a natural response for deliverance, it is powerful, and the Lord yields to the voice of worship. Worshippers must get into the habit of extolling the name of the Lord - this brings major deliverance.

★ **Jude's Deliverance highlights**
- Purity and holiness is God's plan for us in deliverance.
- Worship opens doors in deliverance.

★ **Jude's Deliverance Prayer sets**
- Lord Jesus, cleanse me from inside out.
- Lord Jesus, sanctify my life for your use.
- Lord Jesus, let my worship be acceptable to you.

Book of Jude Learning Journal

_____

_____

_____

_____

_____

_____

_____

_____

_____

_____

_____

_____

_____

_____

_____

_____

_____

_____

_____

_____

_____

_____

_____

_____

_____

_____

Raising a prophetic & curseless generation ●●●

Subscribe to TV, Bible Study and Devotional Plans at

iamuncursed.com

Enroll at our Online School of Ministry

Enroll at the IAUC Online School of Deliverance to get certified as a Deliverance Minister or Prophetic Minister. Get a member of the IAUC Deliverance Ministers' Network

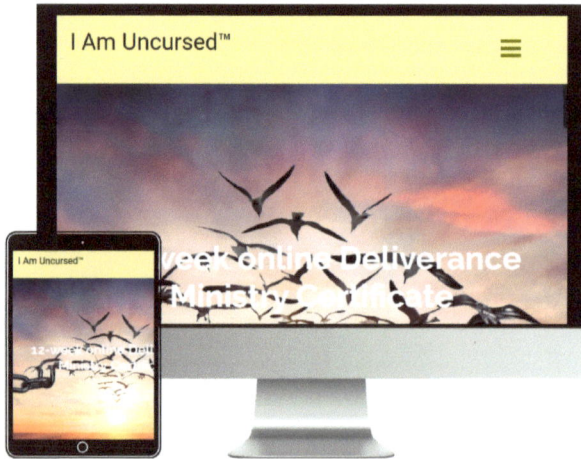

Deliverance for the Deliverance Ministers
Join the Largest Deliverance Ministers' Platform

Marriage Preparation
Or Seeking Marriage Restoration?

Enroll in the Marriage Preparation or Marriage deliverance course

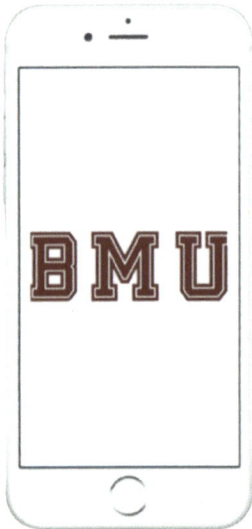

BMU

Blissful Marriage University

MARRIAGE READINESS
AND
DELIVERANCE COURSE

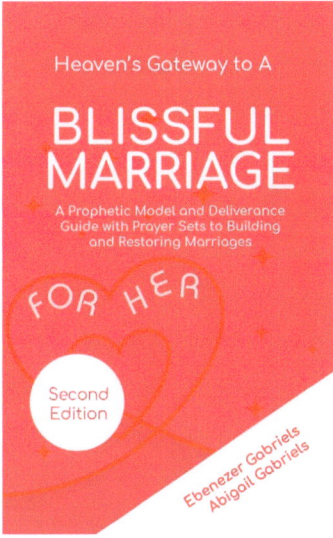

Heaven's Gateway to A

BLISSFUL MARRIAGE

A Prophetic Model and Deliverance Guide with Prayer Sets to Building and Restoring Marriages

FOR HER

Second Edition

Ebenezer Gabriels
Abigail Gabriels

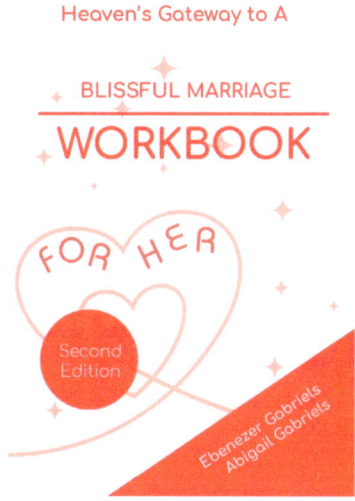

Heaven's Gateway to A

BLISSFUL MARRIAGE

WORKBOOK

FOR HER

Second Edition

Ebenezer Gabriels
Abigail Gabriels

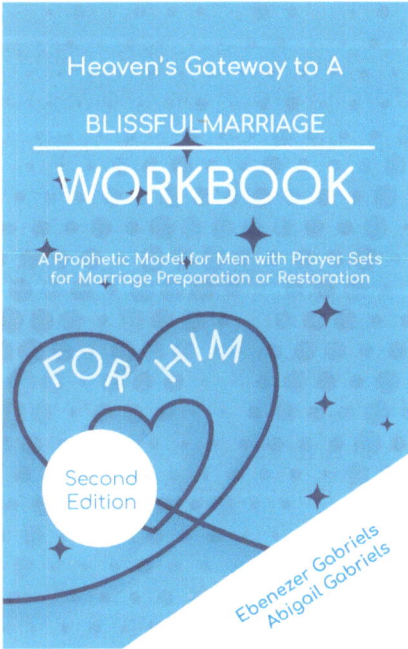

Heaven's Gateway to A

BLISSFULMARRIAGE

WORKBOOK

A Prophetic Model for Men with Prayer Sets for Marriage Preparation or Restoration

FOR HIM

Second Edition

Ebenezer Gabriels
Abigail Gabriels

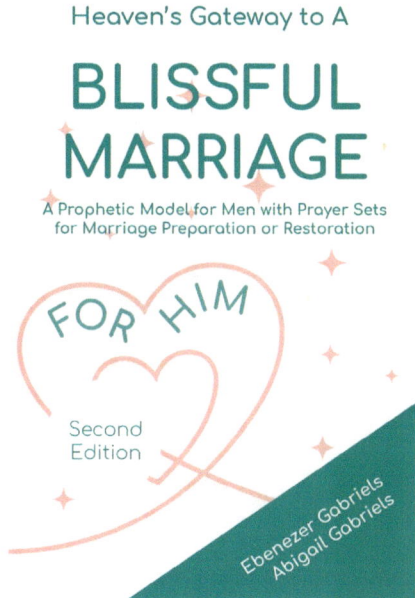

Heaven's Gateway to A

BLISSFUL MARRIAGE

A Prophetic Model for Men with Prayer Sets for Marriage Preparation or Restoration

FOR HIM

Second Edition

Ebenezer Gabriels
Abigail Gabriels

ABOUT THE I AM UNCURSED ONLINE COMMUNITY

A Biblical Deliverance, Deliverance Education and Curse-Breaking Platform

The deliverance of Jesus is here. Uncursed has grown from a stack of prayer pages carried around in a folder, to the Uncursed book available in multi-languages and to the I am Uncursed community, a deliverance and curse-breaking platform. At iamuncursed.com, we are sharing God's Word of deliverance and of power in dynamic ways; through deliverance devotionals, expiration of on-demand deliverance topics and most importantly, Bible study on deliverance. Uncursed is the platform for deliverance discipleship. Ministers of deliverance and seekers of deliverance are getting delivered now, and being equipped for the next season in their lives.

The deliverance ministry is needed across; there are only a few vessels who have obtained the authority to minister deliverance. God is planting His Word into the souls of His people, that they may learn deliverance from His Word and through the teachings of anointed leaders. I am Uncursed is the destination for deliverance discipleship including learning about deliverance for personal growth or ministry growth, exploring deliverance topics, shop deliverance resources and growing in the deep spiritual knowledge of Jesus.

ABOUT THE AUTHORS

Ebenezer Gabriels is a Worshiper, Innovation Leader, Prophetic Intercessor, and a Computer Scientist who has brought heaven's solutions into Financial markets, Technology, Government with his computational gifts. Prophet Gabriels is anointed as a Prophetic Leader of nations with the mantle of healing, worship music, national deliverance, foundational deliverance, complex problem-solving and building Yahweh's worship altars.

Abigail Ebenezer-Gabriels is Pastor, Teacher, Worshiper and a Multi-disciplinary leader in Business, Technology, Education and Development. She is blessed with prophetic teaching abilities with the anointing to unveil the mysteries in the Word of God. She is a Multi-specialty Speaker, with a special anointing to explain Heaven's ordinances on earth.

Both Ebenezer Gabriels and Abigail Ebenezer-Gabriels are the founders of the Ebenezer Gabriels Schools of the Holy Spirit and are the Senior Pastors of LightHill Church Gaithersburg, Maryland.

They lead several worship communities including the 6-Hour Worship unto Deliverance, Innovation Lab Worship encounters, Move this Cloud - and prophetic podcast communities including the *Daily Prophetic Insights* and *Prophetic Fire* where God's agenda for each day is announced and the manifold wisdom of God is revealed on earth. Both Ebenezer Gabriels and his wife, Abigail Ebenezer-Gabriels joyfully serve the Lord through lifestyles of worship and their mandate is to build worship altars to intercede for nations.

Ebenezer Gabriels ministries

ABOUT EBENEZER GABRIELS MINISTRIES

At Ebenezer Gabriels Ministries (EGM), we fulfill the mandate of building worship altars by sharing the story of the most expensive worship ever offered by Jesus Christ, the Son of God and dispersing the aroma of the knowledge of Jesus Christ to the ends of the world.

Ebenezer Gabriels Publishing delivers biblically grounded learning experiences that prepare audiences for launch into their prophetic calling. We create educational contents and deliver in innovative ways through online classrooms, apps, audio, prints to enhance the experience of each audience as they are filled with the aroma of Christ knowledge and thrive in their worship journey. EGM currently operates out of Gaithersburg in Maryland, USA.

CONTACT

Mailing

19644 Club House Road Suite 815, Gaithersburg, Maryland, 20876 USA

iamuncursed.com

hello@ebenezergabriels.org

www.ebenezergabriels.org

Other Books by

Ebenezer Gabriels

&

Abigail Gabriels

Worship

Worship is Expensive

War of Altars

Business and Purpose

Unprofaned Purpose

Marriage

Heaven's Gate way to a Blissful marriage for Him

Heaven's Gateway to a Blissful marriage for Her

Deliverance from the Yokes of Marital Ignorance

Pulling Down the Strongholds of Evil Participants in Marriage

Prophetic

Activating Your Prophetic Senses

Dreams and Divine Interpretations

Deliverance

Uncursed

Deliverance from the Yoke of Accursed Names

Deliverance from the Curse of Vashti

Deliverance from the Yoke of Incest

Deliverance from the Wrong Family Tree

Principles of Prophetic Deliverance

Mind

Deliverance from the Yokes Deep Mysteries of Creation in the Realms of Thoughts, Imaginations and Words

Spiritual War and Prayers

Rapid Fire

The Big Process called Yoke

Deliverance of the Snares of the Fowler

The only Fire that Extinguishes Witchcraft

No longer Fugitives of the Earth

Subduers of the Earth

Prayers of the Decade

Growth and Advancing in Faith

Deeper Mysteries of the Soul (English, Spanish, Arabic and Chinese)

Men: Called out of the Dunghill

Women: Bearers of Faith

New Beginnings in Christ

Wisdom my Companion

Deeper Mysteries of the Blood

Nations and Intercession

The Scroll and the Seal

America: The Past, the Present and the Next Chapter

Herod: The Church and Nigeria

Yearly Prophetic Insights and Devotional

2022 Meet the God Who Saves Blesses Shepherds and Carries

21 Weapons of Survival for 2021

Ebenezer-Gabriels Digital

Communities

Explore the Ebenezer Gabriels Platforms

Deliverance and Prophetic Community: www.IAmUncursed.com

Marriage Community: www.Blissfulmarriageuniversity.com

Children's Learning Community: www.inspiremylittleone.com

Business Leadership Programs: www.unprofanedpurpose.com

Ebenezer Gabriels Ministries: www.ebenezergabriels.org

www.ingramcontent.com/pod-product-compliance
Lightning Source LLC
Chambersburg PA
CBHW041404090426
42744CB00001B/3